MEN are a JOKE

Michael O'Mara Humour

First published in Great Britain in 2000 by
Michael O'Mara Books Limited
9 Lion Yard
Tremadoc Road
London SW4 7NQ

A CIP catalogue record for this book is available from
the British Library

ISBN 1-85479-592-9

1 3 5 7 9 10 8 6 4 2

Designed by Mick Keates
Typeset by Concise Artisans

Printed and bound in Finland by WS Bookwell

www.mombooks.com

What's the difference between a man and a shopping trolley?

A shopping trolley has a mind of its own.

■

How many men does it take to change a lightbulb?

Ten – one to put it in and nine to congratulate him down at the pub.

Stupid man to his doctor:
'Doctor, you've got to help
me. Every morning, regular
as clockwork, my bowels move
at seven o'clock.'
Doctor: 'What's wrong with that?'
Stupid man: 'I don't get up
till nine.'

**Why are mother-in-law
jokes so simple?**

So men can find them funny.

■

**Why are Catholic men like
British trains?**

They never pull out in time.

What goes in dry, comes out wet and gives a lot of satisfaction?

A tea-bag.

When is the safest time for sex?

When your husband's away.

■

'Mummy, what's an orgasm?

'I dunno love, ask your dad.

A couple decided to smuggle a skunk into the country. When they got to the Customs desk the creature tried to struggle out of the suitcase. 'Quick,' said the wife to the husband, 'stuff it down your pants.' 'What about the smell?' he said. 'Well, if it dies, it dies,' she replied.

**My boyfriend's got
a photographic brain –
it never developed.**

There are three types of men:
Tri-weekly, Try weekly,
and Try weakly.

Men fantasize about being
in bed with two women.
Women fantasize about it too
because at least they'll have
someone to talk to when
he falls asleep.

Why do women still like to have a man around?

Because vibrators can't mow the lawn.

■

What's six inches long and gets women excited?

A £50 note.

Did you ever hear about the man who said he could have any woman he pleased?

Shame he never pleased any.

■

What's the difference between the M1 and a boring man?

You can turn off the M1.

D'you think my body's dynamite?' asked Mr Wonderful. 'Possibly,' she replied, 'but it's a shame it's got such a short fuse.'

C'mon darling, don't play hard to get!'

'I'm not, I'm playing impossible to get.'

■

'Hello darlin', do you come here often?'

'No, and now that I know you're here I won't come at all.'

Having undressed for a first night of passion, Mr Wonderful stood admiringly in front of the mirror. 'I had to fight hard for this body, you know,' he said. 'Oh yeah?' she said, bored. 'Shame you lost.'

Why won't a man put a woman on a pedestal once he's married her?

Because, on a pedestal, women can't reach to clean the floor.

■

What's the quickest way for a woman to lose 12 stone of unwanted fat?

Divorce him.

Marriage is a good way for a woman to spend her time until the right man comes along.

What's the real reason men can't communicate?

It's hard to talk and drink beer at the same time.

■

What do you give the man who has everything?

Penicillin.

How can you tell if a man has animal magnetism?

He attracts fleas.

■

What do you say to a man who doesn't believe in free love?

'That'll be fifty quid please.'

Men's first experience of life
is trying to get out of a
woman's body and then they
spend the rest of their lives trying
to get back in.

A man I met in a bar said he was a late-starter. His father's stories about the birds and the bees were so interesting he was 38 before he got interested in women.

Husband: 'Why don't you ever tell me when you have an orgasm?'

Wife: 'Because you're never there.'

■

'What's the definition of a faithful husband?

One whose alimony cheques arrive on time.

My husband's very sensitive about his hair – I don't know why because he hasn't got any.

My husband died at sea.
He would have sent out an SOS
but he couldn't spell it.

■

I met my husband at a dance
and he was the best-looking
man on the floor... I can see
him now, lying there.

This man heard the country
was at war – so he moved
to the city.

■

My husband added some
magic to our marriage –
he disappeared.

Why are men like bank accounts?

One day they're up, the next they're down, and most of the time they show no interest.

■

'Do you think my husband's ugly?'

'Well not exactly, but he's got the perfect face for radio.'

What usually happens when a man puts his best foot forward?

It ends up in his mouth.

■

What do most women miss when they stop being single?

Having sex.

How are men like dogs about housework?

They run and hide every time they see the vacuum cleaner.

■

What do electric trains and breasts have in common?

They're both intended for children but it's the fathers that end up playing with them.

My husband is a well-known
speaker. He can talk
for hours without a note,
and for that matter,
without a point.

My friend Sue has just chucked
her boyfriend because each
time they had sex he said
'This is fun... wasn't it?'

He said, 'What would you say if I asked you to marry me?' I said, 'Nothing, I can't talk and laugh at the same time.'

**You know women's problem?
They get all excited about
nothing – and then marry him!**

■

**Definition of a boring man:
one who, when you ask him
how he is, insists on
telling you.**

My friends said my baby looked just like his father – then they turned him the right way up.

Did you hear about the guy who was so stupid he called in Rentokil because he found a nest of tables in his living room?

**Where can you find the best
selection of men's socks?**

On the bedroom floor.

■

**Why do women have a higher
threshold of pain?**

They need it to put up with men.

A stupid man visited our local museum yesterday and there was a sign saying 'Wet Floor' – so he did.

∎

Plumber: 'Where's the drip?'
Wife: 'He's in the bathroom trying to fix the leak.'

My boss told me he wanted some old-fashioned loving. So I introduced him to my grandmother.

I had to divorce my husband.
He couldn't stand me when
I was drunk and I couldn't
stand him when I was sober.

**What do you call your husband
when he turns up with flowers?**

Guilty.

■

**What do you call a man who
opens the car door for you?**

A chauffeur.

I know this guy who's so stupid
when he wants to count to 21
he has to drop his trousers.

A man heard that most car
accidents take place within two
miles of home. So he moved.

My husband is so forgetful that this morning he stood in front of the mirror for half an hour trying to remember where he'd seen himself before.

More husbands would leave home if they knew how to pack.

■

Did you hear about the man who was so stupid he looked both ways before crossing his legs?

What would a smart woman do if she found her husband in bed with another woman? She'd grab the woman's white stick and beat her out of the house with it.

**Why don't men show
their feelings.**

What feelings?

■

**What is a man's idea of honesty
in a relationship?**

Telling you his real name.

How is an ex-husband like an inflamed appendix?

It gave you a lot of pain and after it was removed, you found you didn't need it anyway.

My husband's great at parties –
he can brighten up a room
just by leaving it.

■

He's not a steady drinker – his
hands shake too much.

Why are men always happy?

Because ignorance is bliss.

■

Why do scientists like to study men's brains?

Because they've never been used.

My man started his career as a
dishwasher in a greasy spoon
café, but he never lived up to
his early promise.

Two men were sitting in a bar and one was complaining to the other: 'My girlfriend says I'm a lousy lover, but I don't agree. After all, how can you make a judgement like that in two minutes?

What do you call a man who tidies up after himself?

An over-achiever.

Did you hear about the guy who was so stupid he thought monogamy was what sideboards were made of?

Why is it no use for a woman to tell a man to get lost?

Because most of them already are.

■

Why do men have an inferiority complex?

Because they are.

**What's a man's idea of
a balanced diet?**

A hamburger in each hand.

■

**How do you stop a man
from drowning?**

Take your foot off his head.

Why do men complain women have no sense of humour when they have no sense and even less humour?

Did you hear about the guy who thought that manual labour was a Spanish trade union official?

**When confronted by two evils,
choose the handsomest one.**

■

**Three wise men?
You've got to be joking!**

**Be kind to animals –
hug a man today.**

■

**Going to bed with some men
can lead to a foetal error.**

Did you hear about the stupid man who was so argumentative he wouldn't even eat food that agreed with him?

No one could accuse
my husband of
being two-faced. If he were
he would hardly be wearing
the one he's got now.

**How many men does it take
to change a lightbulb?**

Who cares, you can never get
them to do anything anyway.

■

**Why did the man cross
the road?**

Who knows why they do anything?

My husband's not all bad – he's a very modest man, but then he's got a lot to be modest about.

**My husband's so bad at
geography he thinks
El Salvador is a Mexican
bullfighter.**

**How did the stupid man
burn his face?**

He went bobbing for chips.

■

**What did your boyfriend get
on his IQ test?**

Drool.

'Mummy, mummy, now that I'm 14, can I start wearing a bra?'

'Shut up, Henry, you're a boy.'

■

What's a man's idea of helping around the house?

Putting the toilet seat down.

**If small is beautiful my husband
is a phallic thimble.**

■

**My husband is a self-made man
and he worships his creator.**

There are only two things my boyfriend can't stand – sexism, and women who insist on being treated as equals.

Did you hear about the stupid man who thought innuendo was an Italian suppository?

What's the difference between men and chimps?

One is hairy, smelly and scratches his bum. The other is a chimp.

Sex with a man is all right
but it's not as good as
the real thing.

■

My husband's so stupid he
thinks fellatio is a character
in Hamlet.

My husband's so stupid he
thinks mutual orgasm
is an insurance company.

This man snored so loudly he
used to wake himself up,
so he started sleeping in
the next room.

**What is a woman's favourite
piece of household equipment?**

A husband with a large bank
account.

■

**What's the definition of
a perfect man?**

One with a 12-inch tongue and
a wallet to match.

**What's the difference between
men and bananas?**

Some women like bananas.

■

**What is a woman's best cure
for loneliness?**

Being single.

Did you hear about the man who was so stupid he thought coq au vin was sex in a truck?

Man: Doctor, doctor, I haven't been myself lately.

Doctor: Sounds like a great improvement.

Why do married women make great comedians?

They're used to getting no response.

■

What's the difference between a man and a book of sexual etiquette?

About 20,000 words.

'My boyfriend's got Hermes.'

'Surely you mean Herpes?'

'No, he's the carrier.'

Wife: 'Shall I cut your sandwich into two or four pieces?'

Husband: 'Better make it two – I couldn't manage four.'

■

Did you hear about the stupid man who tried to get high on coke?

The bubbles kept going up his nose.

My husband's mind is like
a Welsh railway –
one track and dirty.

■

Don't go to bed angry –
stay up and fight.

'How long can a man live without a brain?'

'That depends – how old's your husband?'

Men don't get excited about women's minds – they get excited about what they don't mind.

How do men define an equal relationship?

You cook, they eat; you tidy, they mess up; you nurse, they're taken care of.

■

What's the definition of a tragedy?

Marrying a man for love and then discovering that he has no money.

What's the difference between a puppy and a new husband?

After two years, the dog is still pleased to see you.

■

Why do women cry at weddings?

You'd cry too if you knew the men they're marrying.

I knew a man once whose ambition was to be the last man on earth so he could find out if all those women were telling the truth.

'What have you got in common with your husband?'

'We were both married on the same day.'

**Better to have loved and lost
than to have spent your whole
damn life with him.**

■

**Marriage is a fine institution,
but who wants to live in
an institution?**

I can talk to my husband about any subject I like ... he won't understand it, but I can talk to him.'

What does it mean to come home to a man who'll give you some love and tenderness?

You're in the wrong house.

■

What's the kindest thing you can say about men?

They're bio-degradable.

Woman: 'Do you file your nails?'

Man: 'No, I cut them off and
throw them away.'

■

Why do men act like idiots?

Who says they're acting?

Why can't men make ice-cubes?

They can't find the recipe.

■

What do you call an intelligent, sensitive man?

Extinct.

Man: 'Doctor, doctor, what's wrong with me?'

Doctor: 'You're mad.'

Man: 'Ha! I want a second opinion.'

Doctor: 'All right, you're stupid as well.'

What word best describes most of the men in singles bars?

Married.

■

What's the difference between a man and a chocolate bar?

A chocolate bar will satisfy a woman every time.

**What's the difference between
a man and a gorilla?**

A gorilla doesn't leave so much
hair in the bath.

■

**How do you find out what life is
like without a man around.**

Get married.

**What is a man's idea of a
seven-course meal?**

A burger and a six-pack.

■

**What's the difference between
a husband and a lover?**

About four hours.

How many men does it take to dirty the whole kitchen when cooking a meal?

One.

Women don't smoke after sex because one drag a night is enough.

My husband's at home recovering from a freak accident – he was suddenly struck by a thought.

**What's the difference between
an intelligent man and a
stupid man.**

Nothing, they both think they
know everything.

■

**How many men does it take to
change a roll of loo paper?**

Don't know – it's never happened.

**After 20 years of marriage
I'm finally developing an
attachment for my husband –
it fits over his mouth.**

He makes love like he drives his car – he goes too fast and gets there before anyone else.

**What's the difference between
a man and a tomato?**

A tomato isn't a real vegetable.

■

**How can you tell if a man
is lying?**

His lips are moving.

Did you hear about the dyslexic bloke who went to a toga party dressed as a goat?

■

Never touch a man who says he'll grow on you – he'll give you warts.

My husband and I divorced on the grounds of irreconcilable differences: he's a man and I'm a woman.

STUPID MEN
QUIZ

The Stupid Men Quiz

is published as a public service. It is designed to help innocent young women recognize a stupid man at 50 paces and take action to avoid him.

Of course we all know men are stupid, and EC regulations recognize this by insisting that males should be stamped with an official health warning or, better still, stamped out.

Cerebrally challenged British males, so-called 'beefcake', cannot now be exported and are classed as 'dumb animals'. If you've got one of these and find yourself frothing at the mouth, you only have yourself to blame.

All women should take the Stupid Men Quiz before selecting a man so they can indulge in safe sex. Men like to score with women, but, if **you** score less than 50% in this test, you ought not be permitted to choose a male partner.

GENERAL QUESTIONS

On the following pages are
multiple choice questions,
each with three possible
answers. Tick the box
under the most appropriate
answer, and add up the
numbers beside your
choices to see how
you scored.

**1. Why does a stupid man
never clean out his ears?**

1 Because he can't find them.

2 Because he's growing carrots
in them.

3 Because his head will cave in.

2. How does a stupid man make sex more interesting?

1 He puts a bag over his head.

2 He does it in the next room.

3 He leaves town.

3. When confronted with yet another failure, what does a stupid man do?

1 Pretends that success is for sissies.

2 Gets his Mum to stand up for him.

3 Blames it on a woman.

4. Why is a stupid man like a cheap bottle of wine?

1 He looks good on the outside, but is disappointing once you get him home.

2 He makes you want to throw up.

3 They're both lousy liquors.

5. Why is a stupid man like old age?

1 Neither has many advantages.

2 They both make women depressed.

3 They both come too soon.

6. What do you give a stupid man who has everything?

1 Your hand in marriage.

☐

2 More shelves.

☐

3 Penicillin.

☐

7. You come home to a warm, loving welcome because:

1 You've swapped your stupid man for a dog.

2 Your mother's come round to visit.

3 You're in the wrong house.

8. You know your husband is faithful if:

1 You have him electronically tagged.

2 He's so ugly no one else would have him.

3 The alimony cheques arrive on time.

9. How do you stop a stupid man getting into your home?

1 Move.

☐

2 Change the house or apartment number.

☐

3 Replace the door locks with bra fastenings.

☐

10. How do you get a stupid man to stop biting his nails?

1 Paint them with mustard.

☐

2 Let him bite yours.

☐

3 Make him wear shoes.

☐

11. Why does a stupid man get married?

1 Because he's run out of clean underwear.

2 So that he'll have someone to cheat on.

3 Who knows why he does anything?

12. Why are so many stupid men happy?

1 Because they can't spot irony.

2 Because they're too stupid to realize they're stupid.

3 Because ignorance is bliss.

13. Why does a stupid man like having two women in bed with him?

1 So that he can come and go at the same time.

▢

2 So that he can see double without having to buy a drink.

▢

3 So that they have someone to talk to.

▢

14. How does a stupid man do his laundry?

1 Puts it in the magic basket by the washing machine and waits for it to reappear clean, dry and ironed in his chest of drawers next day.

☐

2 Has it picked up by men in chemical warfare suits.

☐

3 Don't know – he's never done it.

☐

YOUR SCORE

UP TO 15

Oh, dear, you really don't understand men, do you? If you don't wise up fast, the only thing left for you is to become a Tory MP's wife – and you wouldn't want that, would you? Do yourself a favour, become a nun. That's the only way to be free if you're as naive as you seem to be. Do it now, before you saddle yourself with a really stupid man.

16 TO 30

Looks like you're hanging in there by a thread. Get wise as soon as possible or you'll start allowing yourself to be chatted up by some bloke who thinks the erogenous zones are near the North Pole! Get a grip, girl, or, even better, get a life! Remember, no one can treat you like a doormat if you don't lie down.

31 TO 42

Well done, you've got them sussed! There are no flies on you because you've got a cool guy who only wears Levi's buttoned-up jeans. Who taught you? Your Mum? If so, you must be an only child because she'll have realized early on that one drag a night is enough. Keep up the good work!

HOW STUPID IS YOUR MAN?

Here are some more
multiple choice questions.
Tick the box under your
preferred answer, then
as before, add up the
numbers beside your
choice of answer and see
how you scored.

1. Your man's idea of a sophisticated cocktail is:

1 A bottle of Pomagne that is shaken and stirred.

☐

2 Half a pint of shandy.

☐

3 An olive in a glass of beer.

☐

2. Your man's idea of a balanced diet is:

1 Eating on one leg.

☐

2 Leaving the crusts on his egg soldiers.

☐

3 A six-pack in each hand.

☐

3. Your man's idea of a romantic date is:

1 An evening during which he tells you every single little detail about himself, leaving nothing to the imagination.

2 An afternoon at the local football game.

3 Taking you to the pub and actually talking to you.

4. Your man wants to have a special bathtime treat. What does he do?

1 Buys a rubber duck.

2 Invites a bunch of Playboy models to join him.

3 Eats beans for dinner.

**5. When your man takes off his
dirty clothes, he will:**

1 Smell them.

2 Drop them on the floor.

3 Watch them walk out the door
on their own.

6. What kind of exercise does your man take?

1 Chasing after other women.

2 Raising his drinking arm every evening.

3 Jumping to conclusions.

7. What is your man's idea of helping around the house?

1 Going out for a drink so that you are free to clean it all by yourself.

☐

2 Lifting his legs so you can vacuum beneath him.

☐

3 Putting the toilet seat down.

☐

8. If you told your man you wanted to see more of the world, would he...

1 Take you rock climbing?

2 Get you a job as a missionary?

3 Show you a globe?

9. Your man wants to be romantic. Does he . . .

1 Take you to the pub with him?

2 Buy you a dozen cauliflowers?

3 Stop picking his nose?

10 Your man says he's an athlete. This is because . . .

1 He has athlete's foot.

2 He can match Linford Christie's lunchbox.

3 He can dribble out of both sides of his mouth at the same time.

11 Your man tells you he's an animal in bed because...

1 He's small and furry.

☐

2 When he went to the zoo, the monkeys threw peanuts at him.

☐

3 He attracts fleas.

☐

12 Your man says he doesn't know the meaning of the word 'fear' because...

1 He only knows one four-letter word beginning with F.

☐

2 He doesn't know the meaning of any word.

☐

3 He's just plain stupid.

☐

13 Your man thinks he's a wonderful lover because...

1 He sends women into screaming fits.

2 He's faster than anyone else.

3 He practises a lot on his own.

14 Your man is very good to his mother because...

1 She has money and one day he might inherit.

2 He doesn't go home very often.

3 He pretends he's adopted.

15 Your man wants to hold you tight because...

1 He's tight.

2 Otherwise you'd be able to get away.

3 You wouldn't go near him if you were sober.

16 What should your man wear to show off his best features to advantage?

1 A large bin bag.

2 A mask.

3 A smile – he might as well since there's nothing else worth looking at.

17 What does your man remind you of?

1 How easy it is to make mistakes.

☐

2 A headache you once had.

☐

3 The last time you had exploratory surgery.

☐

18 How do you know your man's asleep?

1 He's making a noise like a road-digger.

□

2 You can't – there's so little difference between his waking and sleeping states.

□

3 You can hear his bum snoring.

□

19 What would your man wear if he took you for tea at the Ritz?

1 A T-shirt.

☐

2 Nothing – he's funny that way.

☐

3 Who cares? It'll never happen anyway.

☐

YOUR SCORE

UP TO 20

Liar! No way is your man like this. You're living in a fantasy world! Wakey, wakey! Welcome to reality and the oaf lying beside you. That's better. Now, do the quiz again and do it properly this time.

21 TO 40

You haven't got the sort of man you dream of – he's the sort you wake up with. I suppose he could be worse, but then he could be a whole lot better. He probably boasts that he's a self-made man – and it's good of him to take the blame. He's probably highly class-conscious too – he's got no class and he's conscious of it. There may be something to work on with this one, but don't put too much effort into it – after all, with men, no good turn goes unpunished. Still, having him around is better than haemorrhoids – but not much.

OVER 41

Commiserations – you must have been desperate or very drunk when he pulled you. Let's face it, with his looks he couldn't even pull a chain. He thinks he's got a dynamite body, but he only has a two-inch fuse. He wants to leave his body to science – that's science fiction. The only thing that would get any woman into bed with him is a large blow on the head. Once he got one there, she'd find that he's so useless with his equipment he couldn't even raise a laugh. With his personality you don't need sleeping pills – one word from him and the whole room's snoring. My advice? Take the money and run like heck!

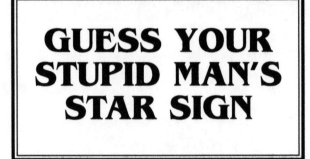

GUESS YOUR STUPID MAN'S STAR SIGN

PISCES

This one's favourite band is Wet Wet Wet. He has a clammy handshake, he's a sloppy kisser and he never seems to need to come up for air. He looks as though his eyes are made of glass and he's a drip all round.

ARIES

He says he can do it like a ram, but actually he's a sheep in wolf's clothing. This one's very woolly-minded and can't do anything on his own. He always follows the flock – usually to the pub. Poor lamb, he just can't understand why the girls don't go for him.

TAURUS

Thick-necked, bullish and with a thing about red, this man needs a ring through his nose and a really good feed. Down at the club he only needs to spy a herd of girls and he charges in with a snort – last one to get to the ladies loo is going to get mounted.

GEMINI

This one doesn't know if he's coming or going! If you find yourself in bed with this one, make sure he's been first! Dr Jekyll and Mr Hyde had nothing on this two-faced git. He's probably told you you're the only one for him – the only one for today that is.

CANCER

This one says he'll grow on you –
yeh, like ivy. He's not at all
straightforward – goes about
everything sideways. He'll sidle
up to you and tell you he's got
something that makes girls go
mad. He means rabies. If you have
the misfortune to catch this one,
throw him back quickly, but make
sure the tide's on the way out or
he might come crawling back.

LEO

This one says he's a lion in bed, but he really means he's a leopard – he's got the spots for it. He's pretty vain – he loves you to run your fingers through his mane and can't understand why you won't. Just because he hasn't washed it since England won the World Cup.

VIRGO

If this one had a pound for every woman he'd made love to, he could buy a bar of chololate now. He thinks sex is dirty, which it is with him because he hasn't washed since he was allowed to stroke Shep on 'Blue Peter'. A night with this one is about as exciting as a party political broadcast, but give him time, he could surprise you . . . by being even more useless.

LIBRA

This one thinks he's a balanced individual because he can hold a pint in each hand without spilling any. There's no justice with this one – either you're wrong or he's right. He's stupid, though. He wanted to be a lawyer and was called to the bar, but lost his way and ended up in the King's Arms. He's still looking for his briefs.

SCORPIO

Ooh, what a poisonous little monster this one is! Who says men can't be bitches? He can never pay a compliment without a sting in the tail. Take no notice of his barbed comments, though. Insects like this have to put others down just to feel big themselves. If he really gets on your tits, just step on him – but make sure you're wearing protective boots.

SAGITTARIUS

A face like a horse and a body like a hippo, this guy's a real animal in bed – he smells, he's covered in hair and he's got fleas. He's got Tarzan eyes – they swing from limb to limb. If you've got any sense, you'll send him back to where he came from – the jungle.

CAPRICORN

What a Butt-head! This old goat will go after anything. Any piece of passing skirt will attract his attention, but once he's got it, he's too stupid to decide whether to shag it or just eat it. He uses a novel form of contraception, though – his personality . . . and that stupid little beard he thinks is so cool.

AQUARIUS

He may think his age has dawned, but that's just because he forgot to put his clock back. He thinks he's a stud, but actually he's just a dud. Women fall at his feet, yes, but that's merely because he hasn't changed his socks in years. He really enjoys sex, though, and can't wait to do it with a woman.

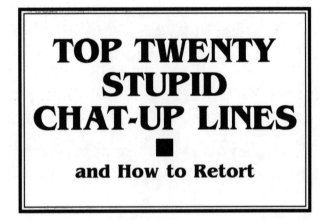

TOP TWENTY STUPID CHAT-UP LINES
■
and How to Retort

Are you a model, darling?

Yes, but you're not a
working model.

■

**Hey, you're not much of a
looker, but I'll have you anyway.**

Thanks, you must be very
open-minded – was that how your
brain slipped out?

Get your coat, love, you've pulled.

If I want your opinion, I'll give it to you.

■

You don't sweat much for a fat lass.

(There isn't an answer – just thump him.)

I'd go to the ends of the Earth for you.

Really? How soon can you go?

■

'Ere, darlin', d'you really want to enjoy yourself?

If I wanted to enjoy myself, I wouldn't be standing here talking to you.

I'm a real lady-killer, see?

Yes, after one night with you they
commit suicide.

■

I'm a carefree kind of feller.

Yes, you couldn't care less as long
as it's free.

Yeh, babe, couldn't you just go for me?

Why – can't you go for yourself?

■

I've got the body of a prize fighter.

Isn't he rather annoyed about that?

I've got something that makes girls go mad.

What's that then? Rabies?

■

Do you kiss with your eyes closed?

I would if I were kissing you.

You're just playing hard to get.

Well, at least one of us is hard –
and I'm playing impossible to get.

■

**That's a great dress, but it
would look better on my
bedroom floor.**

No, there wouldn't be any room
with all your two-year-old pants.

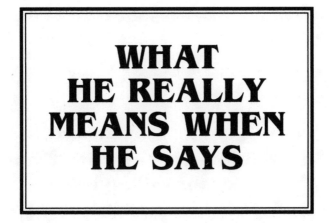

**WHAT
HE REALLY
MEANS WHEN
HE SAYS**

You look tense – shall I give you a massage?

(Get your kit off.)

■

It's hot in here – why don't you take something off?

(Get your kit off.)

She's a lesbian.

(She doesn't fancy me.)

■

Basically I'm looking for a meaningful relationship.

(I want to get laid.)

I'd like us still to be friends.

(I'm going to disappear and you'll
never hear from me again.)

■

I'm separated from my wife.

(She's at home with the children
and I'm here.)

I'm sorry ...

(... that you caught me.)

■

Can I get you another drink?

(Can I get you so drunk you'll shag
anyone – even me?)

I'll phone you.

(You'll never hear from me again.)

■

I'm not ready for a relationship.

(. . . with you.)

What colour do you think I should paint my new flat?

(Come back to my place and get laid.)

■

I'm on my way.

(I completely forgot I was supposed to come round.)

What do you want for your birthday?

(I've just found out it's tomorrow.)

■

You'll never guess what I've just heard.

(Quick, think of something to take her mind off how late I am.)

I need some space.

(Aaaaargh! You want to
get married and I just wanted
an easy lay.)

■

**Let's not talk about me – let's
hear what you think...**

(...about me.)

I would be a faithful husband . . .

(. . . for the first night.)

■

I believe in safe sex.

(I won't tell you my real name.)

**I think women should be
protected...**

(...from doing anything more
interesting than looking after me.)

■

I'm a really carefree guy.

(I don't care so long as it's free.)

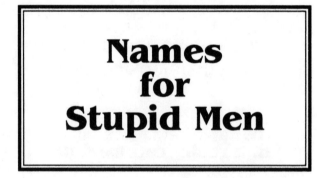

Names
for
Stupid Men

**What do you call a
stupid man with a rabbit hutch
on his head?**

Warren.

■

**What do you call a
stupid man with a
two-inch willy?**

Justin.

What do you call a stupid man with a seagull on his head?

Cliff.

■

What do you call a stupid man with a head made of oak?

Edward.

**What do you call a
stupid man with feedback?**

Mike.

■

**What do you call a
stupid man hidden in a tree?**

Russell.

**What do you call a
stupid man who's just
fallen in the water?**

Bob.

■

**What do you call a
stupid man who sounds
like a lion?**

Rory.

QUICKIES

What is the worst thing about the glass ceiling?

Women are expected to clean it.

■

How can you tell if a stupid man's cooked dinner?

The salad's burnt.

**Why did the stupid man buy
an electric lawnmower?**

So he could find his way back to
the house.

■

**What do you get when
you have two little balls in
your hand?**

Your stupid man's undivided
attention.

What's a stupid man's idea of foreplay?

'You awake?'

■

How are men like flight balloons?

Both are full of hot air.

When is the only time a woman can change a man?

When he's a baby.

■

How are men like dogs?

One stroke and they follow
you everywhere.

How do you know when your boyfriend's really stupid?

When he knows what he wants, but he can't spell it.

■

Why is swapping partners with your friends a bad idea?

It's so depressing when you get him back.

What's a stupid man's idea of fairness in a relationship?

Once with a condom on,
once without.

■

What does a stupid man think of circumcision?

It's a rip off.

What's a stupid man's idea of oral contraception?

Talking your way out of it.

■

How is a stupid man like an old record?

They both scratch a lot.

Why does a stupid man only get half-hour lunch breaks?

So his boss doesn't have to re-train him.

■

What won't a stupid man stand for?

A woman on the bus.

**How is a stupid man like the
local council complaints office?**

Both are impossible to get through
to when you need to talk.

■

**What's a stupid man's definition
of boxer shorts?**

Fallout.

How is a stupid man like a set of car keys?

Both are easily mislaid.

■

What's a stupid man's favourite thought of the day?

Look up a friend.

How is a stupid man like the British economy?

They're both in terrible shape.

■

How is a stupid man like a postage stamp?

One lick and he'll stick to you.